BEIJING
THEN & NOW

BEIJING
THEN & NOW

BRIAN PAGE

thunder
bay press

San Diego, California

thunder bay press

Thunder Bay Press
An imprint of the Advantage Publishers Group
5880 Oberlin Drive, San Diego, CA 92121-4794
www.thunderbaybooks.com

Produced by Salamander Books,
An imprint of Anova Books Company Ltd
151 Freston Road, London W10 6TH, UK

"Then and Now" is a registered trademark of Anova Books Ltd.

© 2007 Salamander Books

ISBN-13: 978-1-59223-798-2
ISBN-10: 1-59223-798-3

Library of Congress Cataloging-in-Publication Data

Page, Brian K.
  Beijing then & now / Brian Page.
    p. cm.
  ISBN 978-1-59223-798-2 (alk. paper)
  1. Beijing (China)--History--Pictorial works. I. Title. II. Title:
Beijing then and now.
  DS795.3.P34 2007
  951'.15605--dc22
                                    2007010383

Printed in Taiwan.
1 2 3 4 5 11 10 09 08 07

ACKNOWLEDGMENTS

I would first like to thank Ye Yu and Dr. Fang Xiuqi of the Geography Department at Beijing Normal
University for their invaluable help in Beijing. In Denver, Sue Eddleman of the Department of Geography
and Environmental Sciences at the University of Colorado provided steady and cheerful support for this
project. I would also like to thank Frank Hopkinson and David Salmo of Anova Books in London for their
patient editorial guidance, and David Watts for his excellent "Now" photography. Many individuals helped
locate the historic images used in this book and I would particularly like to acknowledge Willys Thomas,
Susan Guinn-Chipman, Deborah Hollis, Laura Hagel, Raymond Lum, Billie Love, and Kate Weightman.
Thanks, of course, to my parents for introducing me to China and for their unflagging support through the
years. Finally, I'd like to thank Ayn, not only for her fabulous research assistance but also for her enduring
support and encouragement, and Kirby and Maddie for putting up with me through the process.

PICTURE CREDITS

The publisher wishes to thank the following for kindly supplying the photographs that appear in this book:

Then photographs:
Alain Nogues/Corbis Sygma: p. 30. Bettmann/Corbis: pp. 34, 38, 88, 118, 130, 136. Bill Bachmann/Alamy:
p. 114. Billie Love Historical Collection: pp. 102, 104. Charles Denby: p. 106. Corbis: pp. 6, 46, 86, 142.
Donald Mennie, courtesy of Special Collections, University of Colorado at Boulder: pp. 58, 62. Durham
University Museum, Yetts Collection, Durom 1956: p. 64 (Yetts.40.39), p. 100 (40.32). Edward Thomas
Williams: pp. 74, 108. Felice Beato: pp. 8, 10, 124. Getty Images: pp. 36, 84, 90, 134. Herbert C. White,
from the Collection of Brian Page: pp. 12, 24, 32, 44, 48, 50, 52, 54, 60, 66, 68, 76, 78, 98, 122, 126,
128, 132, 138. Harvard-Yenching Library, Hedda Morrison Collection, Harvard University: pp. 92, 140.
Hulton-Deutsch Collection/Corbis: p. 70. Juliet Bredon: p. 70 (inset). Langevin Jacques/Corbis Sygma:
p. 42. Lee White/Corbis: p. 21. Library of Congress: p. 26 (LC-USZ62-78843), p. 72 (LC-USZ62-92716).
Magnum/René Burri: p. 40. Osvald Siren, courtesy of Special Collections, University of Colorado at
Boulder: pp. 14, 16, 18, 80. Time & Life Pictures/Getty Images: pp. 20, 56, 82, 96, 116, 120. Underwood
& Underwood/Corbis: pp. 22, 28. University of Washington Libraries, Special Collections Division: p. 112.
William Edgar Geil: p. 94. Willys Thomas: p. 110.

Now photographs:
All Now images were taken by David Watts (© Anova Image Library), except for the following: Ayn
Schmit: pp. 41, 45. Brian Page: pp. 15, 17, 33. Dallas and John Heaton/Free Agents Limited/Corbis: p. 57.
Dean Conger/Corbis: p. 53. Liu Liqun/Corbis: p. 115. Ye Yu: pp. 19, 81, 87, 91, 107, 123.

Anova Books is committed to respecting the intellectual property rights of others. We have therefore taken
all reasonable efforts to ensure that the reproduction of all content on these pages is done with the full
consent of copyright owners. If you are aware of any unintentional omissions, please contact the company
directly so that any necessary corrections may be made for future editions.

INTRODUCTION

Beijing has been the capital of China for most of the last 700 years. The city sits on the northern edge of the North China Plain, with rugged mountains to the west, north, and northeast. Beijing lies just 35 miles south of the Great Wall, the historic line of defense separating the nomadic cultures of the northern steppes from the settled agricultural life of the southern plains. This location has been one of the most important factors shaping the city's turbulent history. The origins of Beijing go back to the first millennium BC. For a thousand years, as various dynasties rose and fell, the city served as an outpost at the northern edge of empires. Nomads from the north first conquered Beijing in 936, and various tribes fought to control the city for the next four centuries. The last of these, the Mongols, burned the city to the ground in 1215 but later made it the capital of their vast empire stretching from the Pacific Ocean to beyond the Black Sea.

Mongol rule ended in 1368 when Chinese peasants rebelled, and the Ming Dynasty was established. The grand design of Beijing that is still visible today was created in the early Ming period. The city was arranged as a series of nested, rectangular spaces bisected by a central north–south axis. This orderly design reflected established beliefs about the social order, centering on the emperor's role as sole intermediary between humans and the divine. At the center lay the Forbidden City Palace with its walls and encircling moat. Around this enclave was the Imperial City, defined by its own high brick wall. Surrounding this lay the Inner City, enclosed by a massive perimeter wall with guard towers, imposing gates, and a wide moat. Along the southern edge of the Inner City was the Outer City, itself bounded by walls and moats. Overall, this urban fortress encompassed an area of over twenty-five square miles.

The Ming carried out the most ambitious public works project in Chinese history: the extension and reinforcement of the Great Wall. Ultimately, this huge investment failed to save the empire. In 1644, Manchurian armies invaded from the north, taking control of Beijing and establishing the Qing Dynasty. The Qing rulers did not undertake any dramatic alteration of Beijing's basic urban form, but they redefined the social order of the city. The Inner City became the "Tartar City," in which only Manchu could live, while the Outer City became the "Chinese City."

The Qing rulers maintained the isolationist policies of their predecessors, but by the early nineteenth century the colonial powers of the West were knocking insistently at China's door. While limited trade had been allowed since the 1500s, the Chinese were generally indifferent to Western products and did little to open their economy further to Western merchants, who coveted China's tea, silks, and ceramics. Beginning with the Opium Wars of 1839–42, the colonial powers pushed their way into China and forced the Qing rulers to designate several trading ports. When China's rulers resisted these trade arrangements, Western forces laid siege to Beijing in 1860. The emperor fled, and Western armies occupied the city, burning and looting the nearby Summer Palace.

In the aftermath, Western nations were granted a diplomatic presence in Beijing, giving rise to the Legation District in the southern portion of the Inner City, an area whose architecture bears the indelible stamp of Western influence.

Internal corruption, foreign aggression, and popular revolts gradually eroded imperial rule, which ended with the Revolution of 1911 and the creation of the Republic of China. The new Nationalist government faced challenges from independent warlords, the emergent Chinese Communist Party, and from the increasingly aggressive Japanese. In 1937, Japan invaded China and occupied Beijing, controlling the city until 1945.

Civil war between the Nationalists and Communists erupted after World War II. The victorious Communist army took Beijing in early 1949 and made it the capital of the new People's Republic of China. Under PRC rule, the urban fabric of Beijing changed dramatically as the city was rapidly modernized. Most of the Ming-era walls, gates, and towers were removed, replaced by expressways above and subways below. Huge apartment blocks and massive government buildings appeared in the city, while factories and industrial villages were built on the outskirts. The most striking change occurred right in front of Tiananmen Gate, the main portal to the old Imperial City. Here, state planners razed a large swath of the old city and inserted the giant Tiananmen Square, literally and symbolically dwarfing the landscape of the imperial past.

China's economy has grown at a staggering pace since the beginning of market liberalization in the late 1970s. Beijing, the heart of state socialism, has become a key hub in China's exploding capitalist economy. The city's population has soared to fifteen million people; it bustles with activity. The number of vehicles has doubled in the last eight years, jostling for space with some nine million bicycles. The city has sprawled outward in concentric rings from the center, sprouting high-rise housing and business centers, creating clogged roadways and smog.

Beijing's preparations for the 2008 Summer Olympic Games has accelerated its pace of change. A flurry of government and private investment is remaking the city. New development—from architecturally daring buildings to neon shopping malls—is occurring everywhere, supplanting ancient neighborhoods. Meanwhile, the old palaces and temples that draw foreign visitors are being carefully restored. Socially, Western-oriented lifestyles, with their characteristic consumerism and displays of affluence, appear to be on the rise.

Beijing is an ancient and beautiful city that has passed through several abrupt political and cultural transformations, each leaving its mark upon the landscape. This tradition continues as the city is rebuilt in an era of globalization. Modern Beijing is a city of contrasts, where the deeply layered past and the dynamic present collide in dramatic and sometimes surprising fashion. It is vibrant and exhilarating, pulsing with energy and anxious to take its rightful place among the world's most celebrated cities.

This picture, taken by American photographer William Henry Jackson in 1895, looks to the west along the southern wall of the Inner City. The picture conveys the massive and fortresslike character of the wall, reflecting the defensive role it played during many turbulent periods of Beijing's history. The wall followed a crenellated pattern, with notches and juts at regular intervals. The moat that surrounded the entire perimeter wall is at the left, and the gate at Chongwenmen is faintly visible in the distance. The building in the foreground is the southeast corner guard tower. Ming rulers built four of these defensive structures during the 1400s, one at each of the four corners of the walled Inner City. The small square openings in the stone structure allowed archers to shoot arrows at attacking forces from protected positions.

Today the southeast corner guard tower—referred to as the Dongbianmen Tower—is a striking example of the routine juxtaposition of ancient and modern that characterizes Beijing. It is the only one of the four original corner towers that survives to this day. The moat, which separated the Inner City from the Outer City, was filled in during the mid-twentieth century.

Extending west from the tower is a mile-long stretch of the original Inner City wall, one of the last bits of the wall that still remains, providing a hint of the imposing bulwark that once surrounded the city. This preserved section of wall is separated from Chongwenmen (the street in the foreground) by a lovely, linear, tree-lined park.

This view looks past the northeastern corner guard tower south toward the Dongzhimen Gate. The photograph, taken by Felice Beato in October of 1860, is one of the earliest known photographic images of Beijing. Beato was an Italian commercial photographer who traveled with the British army and documented the Anglo-French military campaign in northern China during the Second Opium War. The British and French forces overran the Chinese forts on the Gulf of Bohai in August before marching to the walls of Beijing and entering the city on October 13. Beato's intentions were to produce photographs of the campaign that could be sold in Europe. His images—like this one of the austere exterior facade of the Chinese capital—record the colonial war from a perspective that celebrates the challenges and successes of the British and French armies.

Morning traffic moves along the Second Ring Road, the innermost of four concentric expressways that surround Beijing. This road follows the footprint of the old city walls, forming a perimeter beltway of nearly twenty miles. The city's walls, gates, and towers were torn down bit by bit during the years of the Republic of China (1911–1948). The northeast corner tower was demolished in 1915 to accommodate the construction of a railroad. Most of what remained in 1949 was dilapidated and was demolished in the 1950s and 1960s as part of the Communist government's effort to modernize the city's ancient infrastructure. With the rapid increase in privately owned vehicles over the last decade, the Second Ring Road now experiences frequent traffic jams. It is also the focus of an extensive new construction effort that includes some of Beijing's signature architectural designs. The "wall" of new high-rises pictured here provides an interesting echo of the past.

Felice Beato took this photograph looking west along the north wall of the Inner City in 1860. Presumably, this was taken at the same time and from the same spot as the photograph on the preceding page, with Beato rotating his position ninety degrees. Along the wall in the distance is Antingmen Gate. On the right, across the moat, is the enclosure of the Altar of the Earth. This was one of eight temples surrounding the city that played important roles in the ritual life of the Ming and later Qing society. The emperor offered sacrifices to the earth at each summer solstice in order to ensure good harvests. The French and British positioned their heavy artillery along the southern wall of the Altar of the Earth and demanded the surrender of the Chinese, who complied by opening Antingmen Gate ("Gate of Peace"), allowing the Europeans to occupy Beijing.

The Second Ring Road is to the left, just behind the trees, having rounded the corner and headed west along the footprint of the old wall. The structures that comprised Antingmen Gate are not visible because they were demolished in the late 1960s. The waterway follows the course of the old moat. The moats that surrounded the perimeter walls of both the Inner and Outer cities were generally filled in as part of Beijing's modernization, but many miles have been retained as part of the city's drainage and water management systems. In many places—like the one pictured here—these waterways have also become the focal points of city parks. The Altar of the Earth still exists but it is shielded from view by the long wall of modern buildings that line the waterway. The altar is incorporated into Ditan Park, which houses many services for the elderly.

Another view of Dongbianmen, the southeastern corner tower, looking to the southwest. This photograph was taken in the mid-1920s by an American photographer named Herbert C. White. White was the art director of a publishing house in Shanghai. Construction on this tower began in 1436; it was the largest of the four corner towers. The wall to the left of the tower is the northern wall of the Outer City, which jutted out a half of a mile east beyond the Inner City corner tower. The wide waterway in the foreground was once the terminus of the Tonghui Canal. The canal, built in 1293 during Mongol rule in the Yuan Dynasty, connected Beijing to the Grand Canal and thus to the agricultural heartland of southern China.

Today, Dongbianmen is enveloped by modern traffic. The moat that once occupied this site has been filled to accommodate the construction of the Second Ring Road (foreground), but the Tonghui Canal waterway still exists, beginning just out of view to the left. The train traveling on the overpass is arriving at the giant Beijing train station, located directly to the north of the ancient tower. This station, built in the 1950s, has seen a recent decrease in intercity rail traffic due to the opening of the Beijing West train station in 1996. The older station still handles trains from northern and coastal China, and remains an important bus and subway hub within the intracity transportation system.

This photograph of the southeastern corner tower was taken from the top of the wall in the early 1920s. It was taken by Osvald Siren, a Swedish professor of Chinese history. The design of Beijing's massive perimeter military structures exhibits characteristics that have been the hallmarks of Chinese architecture for several millennia: the brick building is symmetrical in its layout and features tiered overhanging roofs, with upturned eaves and decorative glazed tiling. This tower—referred to historically by Westerners as the Fox Tower—was stormed and taken by American marines in 1900 as part of their campaign to free hundreds of Europeans trapped in the Legation District during the Boxer Rebellion.

The ancient fortress was given status as a protected historical site by the government in 1982, saving it from the wrecking ball. Today the restored tower is open to the public and houses space for history and art exhibits. The entire interior of the building is accessible and offers a dramatic glimpse into the construction details and military strategies of the past. One can also walk along an adjacent stretch of the old wall and take in views of the Beijing Railway Station and the overall city skyline. In the park that runs along the southern edge of the tower is a plaque that commemorates the tower as a symbol of the Chinese people "resisting aggressors" over the past hundred years.

This is a view of the Deshengmen arrow tower and part of its barbican. Each of the Inner City's nine gates consisted of two main structures: a forward defensive arrow tower and a gate tower sitting atop the main wall. These were connected via a semicircular wall, or barbican, forming a protected courtyard space between the two structures. Deshengmen was one of two gates on the north wall of the Inner City; the other, Antingmen, was positioned about a mile east of this location. Osvald Siren took this photograph in the early 1920s looking to the southwest with the moat in foreground. Note that the Deshengmen arrow tower does not have a central arched passageway beneath it. Among all of the Inner City gates, only Qianmen, the front gate, had this feature.

This is the same view of the Deshengmen arrow tower today, framed by expressway overpasses and a construction site. This is one of only two remaining arrow towers out of the original group of nine that once guarded the Inner City wall. This is also the only portion of the barbican remaining in Beijing. The moat is still there, but the gate tower was demolished in 1921.

The Deshengmen arrow tower was granted the status of protected historical site by the government in 1979 and was renovated in 1980. The tower is open to the public and now houses the Beijing Ancient Coin Museum. There is a small, charming urban park just to the north of the tower, across the moat.

Another view of Deshengmen, looking north from the archway of the gate tower. The photograph predates 1921, as Deshengmen was demolished that year; it was the first of Beijing's gate towers to be torn down. Deshengmen and its paired gate to the east, Antingmen, were built early in the Ming Dynasty, when the emperor moved the north wall closer to the city. During the Ming period, imperial troops would leave on their military campaigns through Antingmen and return in victory through Deshengmen. This historic image captures the massive scale and symmetry of the structure. The brick posts in the center of the photograph mark the crossing of the railroad line that encircled the city just outside the main wall. Built during the first two decades of the twentieth century, this railroad line was placed directly between the outer arrow tower and the gate tower of many of the city's old gates.

Here is a view of the Deshengmen arrow tower and barbican today, as seen from the southern edge of the Second Ring Road. The wide expressway takes up the entire corridor that the main city wall and the railroad line once occupied. The perimeter of the arrow tower is now a busy bus terminal, and the roadways surrounding it are thronged with traffic. This is where one can catch a bus to Badaling, the main tourist site on the Great Wall of China, thirty-five miles to the northeast. The buildup of modern Beijing around the edges of the ancient city is visible in the distance.

This aerial view, taken in 1945, clearly shows Beijing's central south–north axis. The view is to the north. In the foreground is the arrow tower of the Qianmen Gate complex, upon which appears a giant portrait of Chiang Kai-shek, leader of the Republic of China at that time. The gate itself is just beyond, perched atop the southern wall of the Inner City. The barbican connecting the arrow tower to the wall followed roughly the footprint of the roads that can be seen encircling the arrow tower in this view. In the early twentieth century, the barbican was removed and arched passageways were cut into the southern wall to accommodate vehicular traffic. The roads on either side of the gate run toward Tiananmen Gate, which guarded the Imperial City. Beyond this, the rooftops of the Forbidden City extend northward to Jingshan Park. The White Dagoba is visible at the top left.

The aerial view reveals the dramatic alteration of the central axis that occurred with the building of Tiananmen Square. Communist state planners razed a large swath of the city and inserted the enormous public square during the 1950s. The square is flanked by two giant buildings—the Great Hall of the People (left) and the National Museum of China (right). At the center of the square is the more recent mausoleum of Mao Zedong, leader of the

People's Republic of China from 1949 to 1976. Many older landmarks are still apparent, including the arrow tower and gate of Qianmen in the foreground and the Forbidden City to the north. Beyond Mao's Mausoleum is the 120-foot obelisk, Monument to the People's Heroes, celebrating the Chinese people's fight against oppression from the first Opium War in 1840 up to the Communist victory in 1949.

This is the arrow tower of Qianmen. Qianmen was known as the "front gate" of the Inner City, so called because it leads directly northward along the central axis of Beijing to Tiananmen Gate and the Forbidden City. This bustling gate was the main entrance to the capital and the principal gate connecting the Inner and Outer cities. During imperial times, the arched opening under the arrow tower was reserved for the use of the emperor alone; all others passed through side gates in the walls that connected the arrow tower to the gate tower. This undated photograph was probably taken in the first years of the twentieth century. The structure in the foreground is a *pailou*, or decorative ceremonial archway. In old Beijing, pailou were built on main thoroughfares and important crossroads. They carried inscriptions that praised moral principles, often celebrating particular local individuals of high moral standing.

Traffic moves around the Qianmen arrow tower, which is currently being renovated. The original pailou is now gone, but a modern version, designed to span the wide street, has been erected in its place. The tower has been reconstructed many times since it was originally built in 1430. It caught fire and was subsequently rebuilt three separate times over a 250-year period beginning in 1610. In 1900, it was destroyed by foreign troops in the violent aftermath of the Boxer Rebellion. It was rebuilt by the imperial government in 1903 but was remodeled again in 1915 when the connecting walls were torn down to make room for modern traffic. The white railing and decorative lintels on the two lower window courses were added at that time.

The arrow tower of Qianmen Gate, viewed from the base of the Inner City wall, looking southwest toward the Outer City. This photograph was taken in the early 1920s, some ten years after the connecting wall, or barbican, had been removed. It shows the area that had previously been enclosed as a courtyard separating the two gates. By positioning archers in front of the main wall, the arrow towers provided additional defensive capability. The barbican was torn down in the early days of the Republic of China as part of an urban planning initiative aimed at reengineering the traffic flow around the gate. The result was the wider street and trolley car line pictured here.

Today, the roads that once ran north to south along either side of the Qianmen arrow tower have been pushed a hundred yards away from the structure. In fact, the tower is now an island surrounded by a broad green lawn, which in turn is ringed by wide, busy streets. There are no pedestrians in this photograph because the landscape surrounding the gate has been organized to accommodate vehicular traffic, creating an environment unfriendly to those on foot. The white barricades pictured here are used not only to separate traffic directions but also to keep pedestrians from crossing the roadways. Such barricades have become ubiquitous in central Beijing, heralding the triumph of automobiles and standing in marked contrast to the walking city portrayed in the historical image. Access to the tower from surrounding streets is gained through a pedestrian underpass.

The gate tower of Qianmen, looking north from the arrow tower. This 1895 photo, taken by William Henry Jackson during the late Qing Dynasty, shows the protected courtyard between the two gates and the ordinary traffic passing between the Inner and Outer cities. On the right is a typical Beijing horsecar, the primary mode of passenger transportation in the city well into the twentieth century. This tower was built in 1420. The architecture of the gate towers was quite different than that of the arrow towers, consisting of traditional broad wood pavilions placed atop a central archway cut into the forty-foot-high city wall. In this style, columns placed at regular intervals along a symmetrical facade support the tiered roof, while walls serve only as enclosing screens. Other traditional features include the upturned eaves and tile roof.

The gate tower of Qianmen today has no remaining relationship to the arrow tower—the two are severed by a river of automobile traffic and white barricades. Instead, the building orients toward the north, serving as the southern anchor of Tiananmen Square. Remarkably, this is the only surviving gate tower among the original sixteen that once guarded Beijing; it sits atop a small remnant section of the old city wall. In 1989, the tower's rich decorative paint, gilding, and tiling were restored as part of a general renovation. It is now open to the public and features an extensive urban history exhibit. From the tower, one can experience the massive scale of the old city wall.

A view north from the city wall just to the east of the Qianmen Gate tower. This photograph, taken on July 4, 1916, shows the funeral procession for Yuan Shikai, the first President of the Republic of China. The building to the right is Zhonghuamen, the first gate in a series leading north from Qianmen along the central axis to the Imperial City and the Forbidden City. Tiananmen, the entrance gate to the Imperial City, is in the distance. Zhonghuamen was a single-story structure made of masonry with a marble base. It had three arched openings and a single-tiered roof covered in yellow glazed tiles. During Imperial times, walls on either side of Zhonghuamen ran all the way to Tiananmen, separating the corridor from the densely settled surrounding district. Imperial soldiers guarded the gate and the controlled space that led to Tiananmen; no one was allowed to enter without permission.

The view from the Qianmen Gate tower today reveals one of the most dramatic transformations that has occurred in Beijing's history. Some of the changes to the central axis were gradual; the narrow lanes heading toward Tiananmen were widened in the early twentieth century, and many older structures were replaced by modern public buildings. The big change occurred in the early 1950s with the creation of the giant Tiananmen Square by the new Communist government, followed soon thereafter by the Great Hall of the People (to the left) and the National Museum of China (off frame, to the right). Tiananmen Square completely obliterated the historic linear path of linked gates, but Zhonghuamen, a vestige of the central axis, nevertheless remained intact—adrift in a sea of public space. It was finally torn down in 1976 to make room for Mao's tomb, seen here in the foreground.

In this 1979 photograph, a soldier stands guard at the entrance to the mausoleum of Chairman Mao Zedong as a uniformly dressed crowd waits in line to view the chairman's remains. Although Mao had wished to be cremated, his body was embalmed after his death in 1976 and immediate steps were taken to create a fitting memorial. Over forty architects from throughout China worked collectively to design the mausoleum, and it was built from materials gathered from every part of the vast country. The building has an undeniably modern look but retains many elements of traditional Chinese architecture: it was designed as a symmetrical hall, or pavilion, with a tiered roof supported by forty-four perimeter columns and eaves that are slightly turned up at the end. Groundbreaking for the mausoleum began just a few months after Mao died, and the building was completed in May 1977.

Today, soldiers still stand guard at the mausoleum of China's "Great Helmsman." They often don't have much to do, because the mausoleum is only open between 8:30 and 11:30 each morning to limit the exposure of Mao's body to the atmosphere. Before the throngs of visitors are allowed in, Mao's embalmed body—encased in a crystal coffin and draped in the national flag—is raised from its freezer beneath the main floor into the Central Hall of Rest. After the last of the visitors has filed out, the body is returned to cold storage. Nearly 110 million people have visited the mausoleum since it opened. At the north and south entrances to the building stand several massive sculptures depicting the Chinese people's struggle for liberation. The structure sits just south of the center of Tiananmen Square, next to the 1958 Monument of the People's Heroes.

This is a view of Tiananmen Gate, the "Gate of Heavenly Peace," as it appeared in the 1920s. Built in 1417 but taking its present form in 1465, this gate marked the entrance to the Imperial City. The rectangular building is situated perpendicular to the main north–south axis of central Beijing and sits on a massive elevated terrace with five arched openings passing beneath. Tiananmen Gate is an exquisite example of Han-derived palace architecture, featuring a double-tiered roof with wide eaves supported by columns, a yellow-glazed tile roof, and richly painted woodwork on the roof beams and brackets. A marble balustrade defines the perimeter of the terrace, and seven marble bridges span the moat that fronts the gate. The carved marble pillar in the foreground is a *huabiao*. These pillars—there were two in front of the gate and two in back—were meant as reminders to the emperor to walk in the path of virtue.

Tiananmen Gate forms the political heart of modern Beijing and features a fifteen-by-twenty-foot portrait of Chairman Mao. Together, the gate and Mao's visage have become a potent official symbol of the entire People's Republic of China, drawing hordes of Chinese and foreign tourists every year. It was here that Mao Zedong proclaimed the founding of the PRC in 1949, and it is here that significant national ceremonies are still held. The gate's political significance, however, long preceded Mao. For centuries, it had been the point of connection between the imperial court and its subjects, the place where imperial decrees were publicly disseminated. Later, the inauguration of the first president of the Republic of China—Yuan Shih-kai—was held at Tiananmen Gate. The gate was renovated in 1969 and is open to the public. It is the only public building in Beijing that still displays a portrait of Mao on its exterior.

In this undated photograph, Chairman Mao Zedong applauds as he surveys a throng of people from the terrace of Tiananmen Gate. The view is along the front edge of the gate, looking east. The low wall on the right is the back of the reviewing stands that face onto Changan Boulevard and Tiananmen Square. Mao came from a relatively prosperous peasant family and was well educated. He helped establish the Chinese Communist Party in 1921 and later moved the party toward a strategy focused on the recruitment of rural peasants rather than urban workers. This strategy carried the Communists to victory over the Nationalists and Chang Kai-shek in 1949. In the early years of the People's Republic, Mao came to represent national unity, the empowerment of the common person, and strength in the face of foreign humiliation.

Today, the exact spot where Mao stood to gaze out upon Tiananmen Square is not accessible. The edge of the terrace is cordoned off from the public by a gold railing and a row of plants, and it is guarded by state security agents spaced evenly along the perimeter. Security on Tiananmen Gate is tight, because the building is one of the chief symbols of the People's Republic of China. All handbags and backpacks must be checked at the ticket booth, and all visitors are searched before entering. Tourists are not encouraged to linger on the terrace. Streams of pedestrians can be seen walking along Changan Boulevard. In the distance, the National Museum of China can barely be glimpsed across Tiananmen Square through the hazy air.

In this 1966 photograph, Tiananmen Gate is enveloped in a sea of humanity at a rally of the Red Guard. The view is northwest toward the old Imperial City, and Chairman Mao Zedong is riding in the military vehicle at the front of the parade surrounded by thousands of ardent followers. The Red Guard was a militia composed mostly of students and other young people. It was established by Mao in 1966 to help him regain control of the Chinese Communist Party after some of his policies were questioned. The Red Guard was charged with defending the people's revolution by identifying "revisionist" activities among those in authority. The Red Guard enforced strict adherence to revolutionary doctrine, as laid out in a book of quotations from Chairman Mao. In the photograph, nearly everyone in the crowd is waving this "Little Red Book" at Mao's procession.

Today, traffic flows along the vast width of Changan Boulevard, which runs directly in front of the gate, forming the northern edge of Tiananmen Square. Though there are far fewer official political rallies now than during the height of the Cultural Revolution, the reviewing stands are full every May 1 (International Workers Day) and every October 1 (China's National Day). The building to the north of Tiananmen (on the right in the photo) is Duanmen, the next gate along the central axis leading to the Forbidden City. The inscription on the left side of Chairman Mao's portrait reads "Long Live the People's Republic of China," and the one on the right reads "Long Live the Great Unity of the World's Peoples."

This photograph was taken on National Day in 1959—the tenth anniversary of the People's Republic of China. The view is to the southeast. The monumental building in the background is the National Museum of China, which was completed that year. The mission of the museum is to educate visitors about the arts and history of China. The building is a Soviet-influenced Western design, featuring a distinctive colonnaded screen that leads into the entry courtyard. In the foreground, a dance troupe performs the "Lotus Dance" in Tiananmen Square as part of National Day festivities. In Chinese culture, the lotus flower is mainly a female symbol, representing beauty, purity, and fertility. Because the lotus rises up through muddy water, it can also represent rebirth and perseverance. Given this latter symbolic association, it is possible that the Communist leaders intended the Lotus Dance to refer to the struggles of the people's revolution ten years earlier.

As Beijing began preparing for the 2008 Summer Olympic Games, new symbols appeared in Tiananmen Square and just about everywhere else in the city. The large cartoon creatures seen engaging in various athletic events are the "Friendlies," the official mascots of the Beijing Olympic Games. There are five of these Friendlies, color-coded to the five Olympic rings. Four represent animals—fish, panda, antelope, and swallow—and the last represents the Olympic flame. These cute little athletes also represent a newfound marketing savvy among Chinese government officials. The palpable sense of anticipation in the city during this time of preparaton has been expressed by a giant digital clock located in front of the main entrance to the museum, which has counted down the years, months, and days to the opening festivities of the 2008 Summer Olympics.

This 1964 photograph, taken by René Burri, shows two giant portraits set in front of the Great Hall of the People on the west side of Tiananmen Square. On the left is Vladimir Lenin, and on the right is Joseph Stalin. These portraits were matched by two other portraits located in front of the National Museum of China on the east side of the square: one of Karl Marx and one of Freidrich Engels. For many years, these images of the ideological forebears of the Chinese Communist Party were displayed on occasions of great importance to the People's Republic. A fifth portrait in this group—that of Sun Yat-sen, father of the 1911 Chinese Revolution—was usually placed in the middle of the square. All of their eyes appeared to be fixed on Tiananmen Gate and the portrait of Chairman Mao, emphasizing Mao's position within the great pantheon of revolutionary leaders.

The Great Hall of the People as it appears today. The building was completed in 1959, and like the National Museum—its counterpart across Tiananmen Square—it bears the imprint of modern Western architecture in terms of its massing and decoration. The design is often referred to as the "Soviet style" because of its overwhelmingly monumental scale, which dwarfs, and perhaps intimidates, the individual people that it is intended to serve. Though often portrayed as monolithic and austere by Westerners, the building has a majestic beauty admired by people throughout China. The Great Hall is used for legislative and ceremonial activities. It has an auditorium with nearly 10,000 seats—more than enough to accommodate the entire National People's Congress—and a banquet hall with a capacity of 5,000.

Tiananmen Square, June 3, 1989. As dusk falls, students with their bicycles pause, gazing hesitantly at the massing of soldiers along Changan Boulevard, just to the west of Tiananmen Gate. This was the culmination of months of student protests in the square. The protests began as a gathering to mourn the death of a popular reformist politician but soon evolved into a much broader confrontation with Communist Party leaders centered on student demands for greater democratic involvement in public policy. The students had broad support within the city and were joined in the square by urban workers and other activists. There was fierce debate within the party over how to respond to the protest, but ultimately the hard-line view prevailed. Martial law was declared on May 30, and on the night of June 3 tanks and infantry were sent into Tiananmen Square to disperse the protesters.

Today there is no sign of this protest and no marker or memorial to commemorate the event or the deaths that occurred when the protest was violently squashed. In fact, this site could house memorials to additional political tumult. After the Revolution of 1911, there were dozens of antigovernment protests and political rallies in the area in front of Tiananmen Gate. The area became a contested space as protesters and government officials fought over whose voices would be heard. After

1949, Tiananmen Square took shape as the main symbol of the Communist state—a space reserved exclusively for celebration and acclamation of the party line. Nevertheless, struggles to use the square for different political purposes have continued, most notably in 1976, following the death of Zhou Enlai, and in the protests of 1989. While China's economy has dramatically transformed in recent decades, it is clear that its system of political power is changing at a more measured pace.

Duanmen Gate—the "Upright Gate"—is located just to the north of Tiananmen Gate along Beijing's central axis. It is the last gate before coming to the giant Wumen, the entrance gate to the Forbidden City. This photograph, taken in the mid-1920s, shows a portion of the gate and a large expanse of the walled courtyard that separated Duanmen from Tiananmen. The two gates are virtually identical. Like Tiananmen, Duanmen sits on an elevated terrace edged by marble balustrades. Though not visible in this picture, five arched passageways run through this base. The pavilion on top of the base has the same graceful tiered roof as Tiananmen and the same ten columns and nine bays along the long facade. This photograph was taken a decade after the end of imperial rule, when the gate and courtyard had fallen into a state of disrepair.

Today, the courtyard in front of Duanmen Gate is incredibly active; most tourist itineraries lead people toward the Forbidden City through the central passageway beneath Tiananmen Gate and then on through the passageway beneath Duanmen Gate. The courtyard also houses an elite military unit charged with ceremonial duties. These soldiers' daily roles include raising and lowering the national flag in Tiananmen Square. This flag ceremony is a solemn ritual of great national importance. Each morning and evening, corresponding exactly to the time of the sunrise and sunset, the soldiers march out to the square through Tiananmen Gate and across Changan Boulevard to the flagpole. Traffic on Changan Boulevard is stopped to accommodate their passage. This precise military drill attracts large crowds of Chinese visitors every morning and evening.

This is an overview of Wumen—the "Meridian Gate"—taken from the top of Duanmen looking north. Wumen is the front door of the Forbidden City, the innermost enclave of imperial China where the emperor and his court were housed. It is the largest and most spectacular of the gate structures along the central axis. The building is arranged on a large U-shaped base, with the two arms of the "U" extending south to define the central entry courtyard. On top of the base are five separate pavilions representing the five cardinal Confucian virtues: humanity, refinement, justice, education, and trust. This photograph was taken in 1901 after Western and Japanese troops had taken control of the city in the aftermath of the Boxer Rebellion. Pictured is a ceremony honoring the German Count Waldersee, who had negotiated a peace accord with the imperial government, but only after allowing widespread looting of Beijing by allied forces.

Today, the impressive route leading from Duanmen Gate to Wumen Gate is lined with trees, not foreign soldiers. There are plenty of foreigners afoot, but the vast majority of tourists flocking into the Forbidden City are Chinese. Concession stands line the route, and hawkers accost travelers at each step, selling everything from miniature Chinese flags to noisy toys to bicycle-rickshaw rides. The growth of China's economy has led to a rising standard of living in most parts of the country, allowing more Chinese people to travel than in decades past. People come from every part of China to see Beijing's main tourist sites; many are seeing these treasured relics of their cultural heritage for the very first time.

This is an overview of the imposing and mysterious Forbidden City from the terrace of the White Dagoba, located in the royal gardens of the Imperial City. The photograph was taken in the mid-1920s, and the view is to the southeast. The Forbidden City was built over a fourteen-year period starting in 1406, requiring the labor of 200,000 men. The complex is a large rectangle, bounded by a wide moat and surrounded by thirty-five-foot-high walls with guard towers placed at each of the four corners. In the foreground is the northwest corner guard tower, and characteristic yellow rooftops of the palace complex extend far into the distance. The Forbidden City covers 178 acres. It contains 800 buildings and nearly 9,000 separate rooms where the emperors and their families lived a life completely apart from those they ruled.

It is remarkable to see how unchanged the view of the Forbidden City remains today. Its beautiful burnished golden rooftops look much as they did a century ago, though the intervening years took a toll that has necessitated much restoration work—sharply highlighted here by the jarring sight of the large tents enclosing the Gate and Hall of Supreme Harmony at right.

The Chinese effort to maintain this extensive and unique cultural site is significant and has required a considerable outlay of public funds. Equally remarkable is the stark contrast between the ancient complex and the backdrop of modern buildings.

This photograph of the southwest corner tower of the Forbidden City dates from the mid-1920s. It was taken looking north across the palace moat from what was at that time called Central Park. The park sat just to the west of the city's central axis between the Tiananmen and Wumen gates. During the Qing Dynasty, these were pleasure gardens reserved for royal use alone.

Parks for the common people simply did not exist. After the Revolution of 1911, this area was converted into Beijing's first public park. The bridge in the foreground led from the park across the moat to the walkway that ringed the Forbidden City, between the wall and the moat.

Today, the perimeter wall, guard towers, and moat of the Forbidden City are entirely intact, and one can stroll on the encircling walkway. Access to the walkway, however, must now be gained from a different location because the bridge that once spanned the moat at this corner of the palace wall has been removed. After the Communist Revolution, Central Park was renamed Sun Yat-sen (Zhongshan) Park. Though it is directly adjacent to the bustling tourist corridor connecting Tiananmen Gate to Wumen Gate, the park remains a retreat of sequestered gardens and quiet promenades lined with ancient cedars. The paddleboats in the foreground can be rented for moat excursions.

The inside of the Forbidden City as it appeared in the mid-1920s. This palace was "forbidden" in that only members of the imperial household could enter without the permission of the emperor. The Forbidden City was divided into two main parts, the Outer Courtyard and the Inner Courtyard. The Outer Courtyard includes the southern and central portions of the complex and centers on three large halls, used by the Ming and Qing emperors for more public ceremonial purposes. The Inner Courtyard centers on three large palaces, used for the more private day-to-day affairs of state, as well as the residential quarters of the emperor, his family, and servants. The view in this photograph is to the north from the terrace of Wumen overlooking the Gate of Supreme Harmony (Taihemen) and, beyond that, the Hall of Supreme Harmony (Taihedian)—the first of the three great halls of the Outer Courtyard.

The Forbidden City today is officially known as the Palace Museum. It was listed as a World Heritage Site in 1987 and, according to UNESCO, it represents the largest collection of preserved wooden structures in the world. On average, more than 10,000 people tour the museum each day, yet the immense scale of the first courtyard spaces overwhelms even this flow of visitors, making them appear as a mere trickle passing across a vast plain. This impression of grandeur is accentuated by the complete lack of vegetation throughout the Inner Courtyard. Many of the main buildings of the Forbidden City are undergoing restoration. This is the first significant restoration work to occur in a century, and it is being carried out in preparation for the 2008 Summer Olympic Games.

The magnificent Wumen Gate, viewed from just inside the Forbidden City. This photograph is looking southwest and was taken from the raised platform that ran along either side of the courtyard separating Wumen from the Gate of Supreme Harmony. In the foreground is the Golden Water River. This waterway, lined by white marble balustrades, runs from the northwest corner of the Forbidden City southward along the west side of the complex before crossing the width of this courtyard and eventually arriving at the southeast corner of the complex. Directly outside of Wumen are five marble bridges that cross the curving river.

This is perhaps one of the least altered scenes in all of Beijing. In fact, the Forbidden City today has a rather lonely, even eerie, quality about it. The people who once inhabited these spaces and gave it life are gone from history, leaving a giant, well-preserved ghost town. It was almost not to be. During the heat of the Cultural Revolution, the Red Guard demolished historical sites throughout the country. They targeted the Forbidden City, but Premier Zhou Enlai intervened in the Red Guard's plans. He ordered all gates to the city shut and sent troops to guard the complex, protecting the palace from damage and possible destruction.

Taihedian—the Hall of Supreme Harmony—in the winter of 1946. In the foreground is the Court of the Imperial Palace, the largest courtyard in the Forbidden City. After the fall of the Qing Dynasty in 1911, the Outer Courtyard was taken over by the new Republican government, and a museum was established to catalog and display the palace's many treasures. Most of these artifacts were relocated to other places in China for safekeeping by Chiang Kai-shek during the Japanese invasion. In this photograph, students are gathered in front of the hall as part of an anti-Communist meeting at the beginning of the Chinese Civil War. Ultimately, the Communists prevailed and Chiang Kai-shek moved the stash of national treasures to Taiwan.

The Hall of Supreme Harmony is widely considered to be the greatest achievement of Ming architecture. It rises from a triple terrace of white marble and is set off by the expansive Court of the Imperial Palace. Richly painted pillars and brackets support a prominent, double-eaved, yellow-tiled roof. This was the Dragon Throne, the hub of the world, from where the Ming and Qing emperors ruled. The building is undergoing restoration and will be completed in time for the 2008 Olympics.

A view south, taken in 1920 from the top of Jingshan, the hill directly north of the Forbidden City. From this vantage point, the precise geometric layout of the complex is clearly visible. The buildings are aligned north to south with the central spine of main halls and palaces clearly dominant. This physical order reflected the strongly hierarchical structure of imperial Chinese society, which itself was an expression of a fixed, cosmic order rooted in ancient philosophy. At the center of this order stood the emperor, the "Son of Heaven" and the intermediary between heaven and earth, who was responsible for peace and prosperity in the world. China's emperors lived here from 1420 until 1912. The last emperor, Puyi, was required by the Republican government to stay in the Forbidden City, confined to the spaces of the Inner Courtyard at the northern end of the palace. He was expelled in 1924, and soon thereafter the Palace Museum was established.

Looking south from the pavilion on top of Jingshan, the Forbidden City today seems unchanged, save for the green netting and utility roofs that cover restoration work. Beyond the Forbidden City, one can see the National Museum and the Great Hall of the People flanking Tiananmen Square. Both buildings are ringed by red flags placed upon their roofs. On the far right, just to the west of the Great Hall, is the city's new National Theater, still under construction. The ultramodern design for the building, created by French architect Paul Andreu, resembles a giant egg made of titanium and glass floating upon an artificial lake. The building stands in dramatic contrast to its surroundings and has sparked a great deal of controversy among Beijing residents.

Jingshan, or Coal Hill as it was commonly called, viewed from the terrace of the White Dagoba in the mid-1920s, looking east. Jingshan is an artificial hill dating from the early Ming Empire. It was built by piling up the soil excavated in digging the moat surrounding the Forbidden City. It is likely that the hill was placed directly north of the Forbidden City—in line with Beijing's central axis—to accord with the dictates of feng shui; the hill provided the palace with protection from harmful influences coming from the north. There are five pavilions on Jingshan: the Pavilion of Everlasting Spring at the top of the hill, and four smaller, double-eaved structures arrayed on either side of the crown of the hill. The gate tower of Choayangmen, on the eastern wall of the Inner City, is visible on the far horizon.

The view from the White Dagoba to Jingshan today shows the dramatic growth of high-rise Beijing on the periphery of the old city. Eastern Beijing, including the Dongcheng and Chaoyang districts, is Beijing's business and commercial hub, home to international hotels, nightlife, and shopping. It has also become the center of the foreign community in the city. Jingshan, once the highest point in Beijing, became a public park in 1928. The top pavilion houses a large bronze Buddha. In the past, there were Buddha statues in each of the four smaller pavilions, but these were plundered by European troops in the aftermath of the Boxer Rebellion in 1900. Jingshan, known for its more than two hundred varieties of peonies, is very popular with local people, who gather here to exercise, sing, and play instruments.

This is a view from Jingshan (Coal Hill) looking west to the White Dagoba, in 1920. The dagoba is a Buddhist shrine located on Qionghuadao (Jade Island) in the middle of Beihai Lake. Beihai is the northernmost of three lakes that run north to south just to the west of the Forbidden City in the Imperial City. These artificial lakes and hills were initially constructed in the twelfth century but were then greatly enlarged by the Mongol ruler Kublai Khan during the Yuan Dynasty. During the following Ming and Qing dynasties, the area was further developed with gardens, pavilions, and temples. This part of the Imperial City—known as the Western Park—served as a pleasure ground reserved for royal use. It was sometimes referred to as the Winter Palace.

Looking northwest from the Pavilion of Everlasting Spring atop Jingshan. The White Dagoba shrine is still a prominent landmark, but the backdrop has changed with the growth of western Beijing, which now marches all the way into the western hills. On the right is Beihai Lake. Western Beijing is the city's intellectual center, home to many universities and institutes as well as to Zhongguancun, popularly referred to as China's "Silicon Valley." This high-tech district first emerged in the 1980s and has grown on the basis of both private and government investment. There are reported to be over 12,000 science and technology enterprises in Zhongguancun, employing nearly half a million people.

This is a view of the White Dagoba on Jade Island, looking to the north from the Circular City in the mid-1920s. The bell-shaped Buddhist shrine is designed in the Tibetan style. Its dome is topped by a spire and crowned by a canopy of fourteen copper bells beneath a golden flame-shaped tip. It was built in 1651, early in the Qing Dynasty, on top of the ruins of an early Ming-era palace. The dagoba was built to celebrate the visit of the fifth Dalai Lama to Beijing, and to ensure that Tibet stayed aligned politically with the imperial state. In the foreground is the Yongan Bridge, with its white marble balustrades and graceful arched form. This bridge led from the Circular City out onto Jade Island. A large pailou stands at the far end of the bridge.

Jade Island and the White Dagoba form one of the most beautiful sights in all of Beijing. The Western Park, which had for centuries been part of the imperial gardens, became a public park in 1925. In 1961, it became one of the first cultural sites in the city to be placed under state protection, and significant renovations occurred in 1980. Today, Beihai Park is a favorite of tourists and local citizens alike, who rent boats on the water or stroll around the lakeshore. Jade Island is full of winding paths, pavilions, and quiet shaded spaces, leading to the spectacular White Dagoba and some of the best views of the city. The dagoba and its surrounding temples contain many different Buddha shrines, as well as beautiful art tiles and other decorative features. Crossing the bridge is a Chinese tour group wearing matching colored hats—a ubiquitous scene in Beijing today.

Looking east across the Imperial Canal Bridge—Yuheqiao—in the Western Park of the Imperial City. This is a very early photograph taken in 1871 by John Thomson, a British physician. The nine-arched marble bridge crossed the narrow neck of water connecting Beihai (North Lake) to Zhonghai (Central Lake). The bridge was significant because it linked the Inner City to the Imperial City. A decorative pailou marks the far end of the bridge, and the buildings are part of the fortress known as the Circular City (Tuancheng). Though the Circular City was the center of the capital during the Yuan Dynasty, all of the Mongol buildings were destroyed by the Ming, who built their own halls and pavilions in the early 1400s.

The Imperial Canal Bridge in Behai Park today. The marble bridge has been widened considerably to accommodate vehicular traffic, and the original marble balustrade has been replaced by a high metal fence. Across the bridge are the buildings of the Circular City. The main structure in this complex is the Hall of Receiving Light, which houses a five-foot-high Buddha statue.

These buildings date from a reconstruction of the site carried out in 1764. They, along with the Buddha, were damaged by foreign troops in the aftermath of the Boxer Rebellion but were later rebuilt. Two pine trees still growing in the Circular City date from the Yuan Dynasty of the Mongols; both are about 800 years old.

The Drum Tower and the Bell Tower, viewed from the terrace of the White Dagoba in the mid-1920s. The view is to the northeast across Beihai, or North Lake. These two towers date back to Mongol times but were originally located about a hundred yards west of this location. They were relocated and reconstructed in 1420 when Beijing was rebuilt by Ming rulers. The towers were placed on the city's central north–south axis, becoming the northernmost structures along that line. The Drum Tower has been rebuilt through the years, most recently in 1800. The original wooden Bell Tower burned down twice in the eighteenth century. In 1747, it was rebuilt out of masonry and stone.

The view from the terrace of the White Dagoba today. The Drum Tower and the Bell Tower, which once stood out so prominently on the horizon, are all but obscured by high-rise development in northern Beijing. The Drum Tower and the Bell Tower were granted protected status as cultural relics by the city in the late 1950s. In 1980, after significant restoration, they opened to the public.

In the foreground is Beihai Park and one of the boathouses along the lakeshore. Note that one of the pine trees framing the picture is the same tree as in the earlier photograph. Evident in the care lavished upon individual specimens—many are named—is the reverence with which Beijingers treat the venerable trees that abound in parks all across the city.

Two views of the Drum Tower: the first image from 1871 (left) showing its north–south profile, the second (above) taken around 1910 from the east end. The tower is built on a raised platform that supports the massive stone and masonry base. There are eight arched gateways in the base, three each on the north and south sides, and one each on the east and west ends. Directly on the top of the base is the first of three eaves, and on top of that sits a traditional wooden structure with a tiled, double-eaved roof supported by columns. Doors and windows open onto a viewing terrace from all four sides of the second story. The drums were located on the second floor.

The Drum Tower seems simply to be part of the everyday life of this north Beijing neighborhood. There is little formal separation of the building from the surrounding homes and shops that occupy the streets radiating out from the tower; the graceful and beautifully decorated structure sits serenely amid the hustle and bustle that surround it. Because of this intimate setting, the second-floor terrace offers a rare glimpse into the interior courtyards and narrow lanes of the neighborhood. Access to the second floor is on the north side of the building through a steep, narrow stairway leading to the large hall where the drums are played.

This is the view from the second-story terrace of the Drum Tower, looking east over Dongzhimen Street toward Dongzhimen Gate on the eastern wall of the Inner City. The photograph was taken by Herbert White in 1907. The drums on the second floor were used to report the time of day. Originally, there were twenty-four small drums and one large drum. The small drums represented the twenty-four divisions of the solar year on the traditional Chinese calendar. In imperial times, the drums were struck every evening at seven to signal the beginning of the night hours and the closing of the city gates. The drums were then beaten every two hours until five in the morning, signaling the coming of dawn. This custom of sounding the passage of time from the tower continued into the early years of the Republic of China.

The view east along tree-lined Goulou Street shows the dramatic contrast between old and new Beijing. In the foreground are the densely settled, low-rise traditional neighborhoods—called *hutongs*—organized around courtyards and narrow lanes. In the distance, beginning at the periphery of the old Inner City along what is now the Second Ring Road, are high-rise apartment buildings and office complexes. But old Beijing is changing fast. In the right foreground, a hutong has just been torn out and will soon be redeveloped with modern buildings. During the time that the Drum Tower is open to the public, the replica drums are beaten every half-hour in a reenactment of the traditional practice. Historically, these drums could be heard for a mile; now it's difficult to hear them from the base of the tower as traffic passes by.

This is the Bell Tower as seen from the second-floor terrace of the Drum Tower, looking due north. The photograph dates from the early 1920s. Like the Drum Tower, the Bell Tower sits on an elevated platform and is surrounded by a diamond-shaped walled enclosure. The massive stone-and-masonry base has an arched opening on each of its four sides. The masonry second story steps in twice from the base, creating two terraces, the higher of which is ringed by a marble balustrade. The tower is capped by a double-tiered roof. The bell hung from a wooden frame in the center of the second story. It was eighteen feet high, weighed forty-two tons, and could be heard ten miles away. The bell was struck twice each day: once following the drums at seven in the evening, and again following the drums at five in the morning.

Today the setting of the distinctive Bell Tower is simultaneously modern and ancient. This view north from the Drum Tower provides one of the best overviews of old hutongs in the entire city. A hutong is a neighborhood of joined *siheyuan*—traditional Chinese courtyard residences—that are reached along narrow alleys. The residences are oriented inward around the courtyard and turn their backs—often high brick walls—to the street. These compounds vary greatly one to the next so that, from above, the tile rooftops form a jumble of different sizes, shapes, and orientations. In contrast to these irregular patterns, suburban Beijing sprawls northward in an orderly grid filled with high-rise development. Large tour buses now dominate the courtyard between the two towers, indicating that the Drum and Bell towers are on the list of primary tourist destinations in Beijing.

The Temple of Confucius is located in the northeast portion of the Inner City, not far from the Drum and Bell towers. Confucian thought emphasized moral virtue, correctness of social relationships, justice, and sincerity. It encouraged education and continual study. Confucianism won the favor of China's emperors because of its teachings about the natural hierarchy of ruler and subject. This temple was originally built in 1306 during the Yuan Dynasty. Here, scholars prepared students for the rigorous civil service examinations, in which they were required to demonstrate flawless knowledge of the Confucian classics. This photograph dates from the mid-1920s. In the foreground is the courtyard leading to the Hall of Great Accomplishments. The marble steps leading to the hall are divided by a carved slab featuring a dragon and cloud motif. The structure has a double-eaved hip roof with the imperial yellow tile.

The Temple of Confucius is one of two showpieces of the Capital Museum, which houses a permanent collection of cultural artifacts from Beijing. The museum is located on quiet, tree-lined Guozijian Street in the northern part of the old city. This street has two of the last remaining pailou on Beijing's roadways. Today, the temple is screened and scaffolded. Like so many other cultural sites in the city, it is being restored in anticipation of the wave of visitors expected to arrive for the 2008 Olympics. The same cypress trees line the courtyard in front; in fact, one is over 700 years old. At the entry to the courtyard are 198 stone tablets that record the names and hometowns of the nearly 52,000 candidates that successfully passed the exams held during the Yuan, Ming, and Qing dynasties.

The Imperial Hall of Guozijian—the Hall of Classics—photographed in the mid-1920s. The Hall of Classics was part of a school of Confucian philosophy situated just to the west of the Temple of Confucius—it was traditional practice to locate an academy to the right of a temple. It was built in 1783 during the Qing Dynasty on the site of a former imperial college that had been founded in the early Ming Dynasty. The building is a square pavilion with a double-eaved hip roof, covered in the imperial yellow tile, and topped by a large gilded ball. The structure rests on a marble terrace and is surrounded by a moat that is crossed by four marble bridges. Inside, the emperor would deliver his annual lecture on the classic Confucian texts.

The Hall of Classics is the second of the two main showpieces of the Capital Museum, the first being the Temple of Confucius. The two are located adjacent to one another in the same complex of buildings. After the Communist Revolution, Confucian temples and their associated academies were converted to other uses and often fell into disrepair or were abandoned entirely. Today, however, the Chinese government is beginning to honor this heritage and even promote the benefits of Confucian thought. The Hall of Classics is presently undergoing extensive renovation and is covered in scaffolding and netting that masks the building's delicate architecture. But even with all of the construction activity, the hall and its immediate surrounding retain an air of quiet studiousness.

The Mongol emperor Kublai Khan founded an imperial observatory near this site in the late thirteenth century. His astronomers were able to fix the length of the year to within a thousandth of a day relative to modern measurements. Such accuracy was achieved using large bronze astronomical instruments of Chinese origin. During the Ming Dynasty, most of these original instruments were relocated to Nanjing and copies were made for Beijing. The observatory sat on a fifty-foot-high platform located on the eastern wall of the Inner City. This photograph, dating from the early 1920s, is looking southeast toward the observatory platform. The angled wall above the arched opening is the stairway leading to the top of the platform, and the eastern wall of the Inner City is on the left, looking ragged and overgrown.

Today, the observatory survives as a relic of ancient Beijing. The eastern wall of the Inner City that once abutted the observatory was torn down as part of the urban modernization program of the 1950s. All that remains of that wall is the very short section pictured here to the left of the stairway. Renovation of the observatory accompanied the removal of the city walls, and the Beijing Ancient Astronomical Equipment Exhibition Hall officially opened in 1956. In addition to the observatory tower, the site contains a small museum organized around a central courtyard. The exhibits in the museum cover the history of astronomy, and the courtyard features reproductions of Yuan Dynasty astronomical instruments.

The instruments at the imperial observatory sat on top of a platform, ten feet above the height of the adjacent city wall. This photograph, looking out from the top of the platform to the south, was taken in 1946. The southeast corner tower of the Inner City wall can be seen in the distance. In the left foreground is an ecliptic armillary, and in the center foreground is an azimuth theodolite. Most of these instruments date from the 1670s. They were built by Father Ferdinand Verbiest, a Belgian Jesuit, and replaced the older Chinese instruments. Jesuits were accepted into the Ming and Qing imperial courts because of their knowledge of mathematics and astronomy. Father Verbiest was appointed to the Astronomical Board by the Qing emperor Kangxi.

The view from the top of the observatory platform is dizzying. The venerable astronomical instruments stand in stark contrast to the modern buildings that now surround the observatory. At right is a large Marriott hotel, hinting at the vast increase in foreign visitors to Beijing in recent years, as China's rapidly growing economy offers increasing opportunities for foreign investors from around the world. At left is a glimpse of the busy Second Ring Road as it encircles the southeast corner of the old city. Today, the observatory sits at one of the city's most heavily trafficked intersections, but the museum courtyard below offers a small and lovely sanctuary that belies the bustle surrounding the site.

This photograph of the observatory dates from 1871. In the right foreground is an equatorial armillary, and to the left is a celestial globe. The view is to the southwest, and the tower in the distance is likely the gate tower of Qianmen. In all, Jesuit priest Father Verbiest designed six instruments, and he published a record of his inventions, accompanied by illustrations, in Europe in 1687. Because Father Verbiest's descriptions of his instruments had circulated widely in Europe, European travelers to China were drawn to the site and often made it the focus of their photography.

In the aftermath of the 1900 Boxer Rebellion, French and German troops looted the observatory and took the instruments to Europe. The French returned and reinstalled the stolen items in 1902. The instruments taken by the Germans were not returned until 1921. The reassembled equipment was put on public display in 1956. The city has changed dramatically in every direction. This photograph looks west, back into the old Inner City, and shows the concentration of new buildings along Changan Boulevard in the vicinity of Tiananmen Square. This view into the distance highlights the air-quality problems that rapidly developing Beijing faces.

This undated photograph was probably taken in the first decade of the twentieth century. The view is from the arrow tower of Chongwenmen Gate (also called Hatamen Gate) on the southern wall of the Inner City, looking south into the Outer City. Chongwenmen was an important point of commercial interchange between these two parts of Beijing. The street in the foreground is busy with people, donkeys, and carts passing across the moat and through the gate. The low buildings of the Outer City stretch far into the distance. While the street system of the Inner City was generally well ordered and carefully laid out, the Outer City was a jumble of winding narrow streets, shops, and densely settled neighborhoods, or hutongs.

A view south into the Chongwenmen district, at the busy intersection of Chongwenmenwai and Chongwenmen boulevards. The historic gate was demolished in 1959. This photograph was taken from a pedestrian bridge that spans the roadway. This part of the old Outer City has been transformed over the past twenty-five years. Along this thoroughfare, most of the old hutongs have been removed, replaced by modern high-rise shopping and office complexes. The cranes visible on the left attest to the ongoing redevelopment of this district; it nevertheless remains an active shopping mecca. Two blocks down, visible on the right-hand side of the boulevard, is the New World Shopping Center, one of Beijing's modern shopping malls.

Because people of Chinese ancestry were not permitted to live in the Inner City during the Qing Dynasty (1644–1911), they became concentrated in the Outer City. For this reason, the Outer City was called the Chinese City. This was the commercial heart of Beijing, full of artisans, shops, restaurants, brothels, and theaters. Similar types of commercial activities tended to cluster together, and the streets were named accordingly. There was a Silk Street, a Jade Street, a Lantern Street, and so on. This photograph shows Bead Street in the early 1930s. Bead Street was located not too far from the Legation Quarter—the heart of foreign residences in Beijing. The prevalence of English-language signs indicates that the area was frequented by foreign shoppers.

Some of the old commercial streets of the Chinese City have survived, but Bead Street—like so many others—has disappeared. It was located in the eastern half of the old Chinese City, in the Chongwenmen district. Over the past few decades, most of the old hutongs were removed and the area has been thoroughly rebuilt. The apartment buildings shown here are typical of the pattern of new high-rise development, which has included street landscaping and park spaces. These changes reflect efforts by the government to improve living conditions for Beijing residents. Though the hutongs are a treasured vestige of Beijing's past, many were also dilapidated, with inadequate sewer, water, and other services. In contrast, the new complexes have many conveniences, such as air-conditioning. The trade-off between cultural heritage and modern amenities is a source of lively debate among Beijing residents.

This is an overview of Qianmen Boulevard, the main commercial street of the Outer City. This street led south from Qianmen Gate along Beijing's central axis to Yondingmen Gate, the southern entrance to the Outer City. The photograph dates from 1871 and was taken from the semicircular barbican wall joining the Qianmen arrow tower to its gate tower. The base of the gate's arrow tower is visible on the left. The prominent Hall of Prayers within the Temple of Heaven can be seen on the horizon, a little left of center, beyond the expanse of jumbled hutong rooftops. In the foreground is a wide marble bridge that crosses the city moat. Just south of the moat, a large pailou spans the street, which is lined with stalls and carts.

Compared to the modernized eastern part of the old Chinese City, the hutongs adjacent to Qianmen Gate and to the west remained relatively intact until quite recently. This photograph looks south along Qianmen Boulevard from ground level at the edge of the tower. Tall blue construction fences now dominate the view, hiding the wrecking crews that are systematically removing the district's dense maze of narrow lanes and residences. The government's effort to "protect historical and cultural relics" has already removed hundreds of old courtyard homes and shops in these hutongs, sparking an outcry from residents and historic preservationists who believe that commercial real-estate development is the main reason behind demolition. Ultimately, the government wants to relocate thousands of people from the Qianmen district to the suburbs in order to alleviate overcrowding and meet other real-estate demands in the city center. The inset photograph shows a construction crew clearing the area just to the west of Qianmen Gate.

The district just to the southwest of Qianmen Gate has been one of the busiest in all of Beijing since the Ming Dynasty. At the center of this area is Dazhalan Street, famous for its shops and theaters. Dazhalan (meaning "Great Fence") was named for the two barricades that stood at either end of the short lane (it's only an eighth of a mile long). These gates were intended to protect the residents and shops along the street; they were shut every evening at nightfall and reopened each morning. The photograph, dated to sometime around 1940, shows the narrow character of Dazhalan and the elaborate metal gate that stood at the western end of street.

Dazhalan Street today is still one of Beijing's most active shopping hubs, attracting customers from all over the city. It is also a magnet for foreign tourists, who flock to the colorful stores that line the street looking for bargains. The gate at the west entrance to the short lane is gone, but the decorative metalwork from the east gate remains. Improvements to Dazhalan were made recently, and the street is now reserved for pedestrians alone. The row of bicycles on the right is a common sight in this city, where an estimated nine million bicyclists take to the streets each day.

The commercial streets of the Inner City tended to be wider and more ordered than those in the Outer City. This photograph shows Fuchengmen Street around 1910. It was taken from the top of Fuchengmen Gate on the western wall of the Inner City, looking east along a street filled with shops and stalls. Jingshan, or Coal Hill, is visible in the far distance. The tall structure on the left is a Buddhist shrine—the Temple of the White Pagoda. The temple was built in 1271 during the reign of Kublai Khan in the Yuan Dynasty. It has the same Tibetan-style design as the White Dagoba in Beihai Park, but this shrine is larger and much older.

Over time, the streets that led to the nine gates of the Inner City became clustered with shops and businesses. Though the gates are now gone, this land-use pattern continues. Fuchengmen Gate was demolished in 1965 to make way for the western stretch of the Second Ring Road, which is generally thronged with heavy traffic. Fuchengmen Street was widened into a major thoroughfare, but stores still line this stretch of roadway. The White Pagoda Temple, one of the oldest structures in Beijing, gained state protection as an important cultural relic in 1961. Renovation of the site took place in 1978 and again in 2002.

The Temple of Heaven complex is located in the southern part of the Outer City. Built in 1420, it is where the emperors of the Ming, and later Qing, dynasties worshipped heaven and prayed for good harvests. This aerial photograph was taken in 1946, looking to the north. From this perspective, the north–south axis of the complex is clearly visible. To the north is the Hall of Prayers, connected by a long causeway to the giant Altar of Heaven at the southern end of the complex. The layout of circular shapes set within square shapes had significance. Circles represented heaven, and squares represented earth; thus, symbolically, this was the place where heaven met earth.

This ground view looks north from the southern grouping of ceremonial gates visible at the bottom of the historic aerial photograph. The imposing Altar of Heaven is framed by the other set of gates. The temple complex is set within giant Tiantan Park, one of Beijing's largest and most popular public spaces. The park is one of the best places in the city to watch the ebb and flow of everyday life in Beijing. Here, parents stroll with their children, musicians gather for informal concerts, elders practice tai chi, and legions of badminton players whack birdies back and forth. Playfulness and exuberance mark these public pursuits.

The Hall of Prayer is situated at the northern end of the Temple of Heaven. It was here that the emperor came at the beginning of each spring to pray for good harvests in a ritual that dates from the third century BC. The emperor was regarded as the "Son of Heaven" who administered divine authority on earth. All good that happened in the world emanated from him. Conversely, if crops failed or other catastrophes fell upon the country, it was viewed as a sign that he had fallen out of the favor of heaven. The hall was originally built in 1420. It sits at the center of a three-tiered circular marble terrace surrounded by marble balustrades. The building is a circular wooden structure with a triple-tiered roof, topped by a gilded ball. This photograph dates from the 1920s, when the old rituals were no longer observed and the building and its surroundings had fallen into disrepair.

Here one sees the lovely Hall of Prayer thronged with rapt visitors, most of them Chinese. The circular building has been beautifully renovated, painted with the elaborate designs and vivid colors it once displayed. The blue tiles on the conical roof represented the Chinese imagery of heaven. It is difficult to imagine, as one views this masterpiece of wooden architecture, that it was constructed by craftsmen without the use of a single nail. The Temple of Heaven complex was given protected status in 1961 and was designated as a UNESCO World Heritage Site in 1998. This exquisite building has virtually become an icon of Beijing, serving as the signature image of the city on book covers and Web sites throughout the world.

This photograph was taken from the Altar of Heaven, looking north along the axis of the Temple of Heaven complex in 1871. Every year on the day before the winter solstice, the emperor came here from the Forbidden City in a procession of over two thousand dignitaries and members of the imperial court. The ritual of worshipping heaven lasted several days, and on the morning of the solstice, the emperor offered sacrifices and prayers at the Altar of Heaven. The circular altar consists of three marble terraces, each ringed by a white marble balustrade. This ceremony had to be carried out perfectly; any mistakes constituted a bad omen for the coming year and put the emperor's heavenly mandate to rule at risk. Just to the right of the center of the photograph is the small, circular Hall of Heaven. In the distance is the Hall of Prayer.

This scene seems quite unchanged after nearly 140 years. The view is to the north from the third terrace of the Altar of Heaven. Visible through the two sets of ceremonial gates is the circular Hall of Heaven, also known as the Imperial Vault of Heaven, topped with a gilded ball. The Hall of Heaven was built in 1530 and later restored in 1730. It is the sanctuary where the emperor changed into sacrificial robes and consulted the tablets of his ancestors before the solstice ceremonies. The Hall of Heaven is an exquisite building with beautifully painted woodwork and the characteristic blue-tile roof representing heaven. The dragon heads in the foreground are spouts that drain water from the top terrace of the Altar of Heaven.

In the aftermath of the Second Opium War in 1860 and the occupation of Beijing by British and French troops, China's Manchu rulers reluctantly granted foreign governments the right to keep permanent diplomatic representatives in Beijing. The Chinese imperial government first offered several areas outside of the Inner City wall, but the foreign powers were determined to place their legations within the wall. Over the next several decades, the Legation Quarter took shape inside the Inner City. The district lay between Qianmen Gate on the west and Chongwenmen Gate on the east and was bounded by the Inner City wall to the south. The legations were walled compounds with controlled access gates. This photograph, taken around 1900, shows the main gate of the British legation—a Beaux Arts design—probably just before the Boxer Rebellion.

The main gate to the old British legation still stands today. It is one of the few structures in the Legation Quarter that survived the Boxer Rebellion of 1900. The British legation was the largest compound in the district, reflecting Britain's role as leader among the foreign powers in China during the late nineteenth and early twentieth centuries. After the revolution of 1949, many Western nations, including Britain, refused to formally recognize the People's Republic of China. The diplomats from these governments were expelled, and their legation compounds were seized by the new communist state. While some foreign buildings in the district were torn down, many were kept and adapted for new uses. The walled compound of the old British legation now houses the Chinese Ministries of State and Public Security.

The Imperial Canal ran north and south through the middle of the Legation Quarter. The canal drained the lakes and waterways of the Imperial City. This photograph of the canal was taken in 1900, looking to the north, on the eve of the Boxer Rebellion. On the left is the British legation, and on the right is a gate to the Palace of Prince Su, a pattern indicative of the mix of foreign and Chinese occupancy in the district. The Boxers were a group of Chinese nationalists who resented the foreign colonial presence and began to kill foreign missionaries and their Chinese converts. In June of 1900, the Boxers, aided by elements within the imperial army, attacked the Legation Quarter. The foreign community took refuge in the British legation—they were rescued by British and American soldiers after a fifty-five-day siege. Most buildings in the district were destroyed in the conflict.

The foreign community in the Legation Quarter viewed the Imperial Canal as a filthy, bad-smelling ditch. They filled in the canal during the 1920s and replaced it with a European-style public park. Today, this park forms a beautiful, tree-lined pedestrian corridor through the district. The park's flower gardens and many public benches make it a relatively quiet and secluded spot in the heart of the fast-paced city, just blocks from the frenetic Wangfujing shopping district. As with the canal in the past, roads run along both sides of the park, separating it from the storefronts and the walled compounds of various government ministries. The person in orange clothing is a municipal worker sweeping the pathways. Generally, Beijing's parks and other public spaces are clean and very well maintained.

After the rebellion, suspected Boxers were publicly executed and foreign troops looted the city. The foreign powers were granted complete control over the Legation Quarter, which became a city apart from the rest of Beijing. Chinese-owned land within the district was appropriated, allowing the legations to grow in size, while a wall and gates were built around the perimeter. Chinese visitors to the district were required to show "letters of introduction" before being admitted. The streets were widened, streetlamps were installed, and all of the legations were rebuilt. Whereas the old legations had often reflected Chinese styles, the new legations were built in various Western architectural styles that were then popular back in the home country. This photograph, from around 1905, shows Legation Street. To the east, in the distance, is St. Michael's Catholic Church, built in 1902. One of the gates to the French legation is in the left foreground.

After 1949, all of the Western and Japanese street names in the Legation Quarter were replaced with Chinese names. Legation Street was renamed Dongjiaomin Xiang. As this photograph shows, the basic physical character of the district is remarkably unchanged. The streetscape is still dominated by walled compounds that can be accessed only through restrictive gates. The old French legation on the left is now the home of Cambodian king

Sihanouk. St. Michael's church is still there but is obscured by trees and new buildings. The church, like many other buildings in the old Legation Quarter, became a target of antiforeign attacks during the Cultural Revolution and was badly damaged. It was restored in 1989 and is now the Dongjiaomin Xiang Catholic Church.

On the left is the view from a barricade on the city walls showing the Stars and Stripes flying once more over the bullet-riddled American Legation, after its successful recapture in 1900. In the distance are the rooftops of the Forbidden City and Coal Hill. The United States legation sat just to the east of Qianmen Gate. The compound was enlarged and rebuilt following the Boxer Rebellion. The new buildings (above) were designed in the United States and were built from imported American materials. A government architect was sent to supervise construction. The 1920 photograph shows the residence of the ambassador and its surrounding grounds. The eclectic building combines elements of the Colonial Revival and Renaissance Revival styles. The photograph was taken from the top of the south wall of the Inner City, looking to the north. Legation Street runs east to west just beyond the ambassador's residence, and Tiananmen Gate is faintly visible in the distance to the left of the building.

Many of the buildings in the old U.S. legation compound remain today. The southern wall of the Inner City was torn down years ago; this view is from Qianmen Dong Boulevard, which follows the footprint of the old wall. The U.S. diplomatic presence in Beijing came to an abrupt end when Mao Zedong announced the founding of People's Republic of China from nearby Tiananmen Gate in 1949. The compound was appropriated by the Chinese government, and now the former ambassador's residence is a Municipal Police Museum. This scene is typical of the Legation Quarter today; many buildings from the days of foreign presence remain, but very little effort has been put into restoration, reflecting China's understandable hesitation to preserve a landscape that represents a period of domination by foreign powers.

New commercial buildings sprang up throughout the Legation Quarter as the district was reconstructed and modernized after 1900. This included many banks, trading houses, stores, and hotels. This 1920s photograph was taken looking east along Legation Street at the intersection of Rue Meiji, which ran along the east side of the Imperial Canal. On the left is the impressive Japanese Yokohama Specie Bank. This building was designed in the Beaux Arts style, featuring a distinctive banded brick facade. Across Legation Street from the bank is the famous Grand Hotel des Wagons-Lits. Built in the early 1900s, this hotel represented an entirely new standard of Western luxury in Beijing. It quickly became the fashionable place for foreign visitors to stay in the Chinese capital.

The former Yokohama Specie Bank building now houses a Chinese financial institution. The building looks much the same as in the past, save for the "Rising Sun" flag previously perched atop its dome. Curiously, most of the buildings in the Legation Quarter that belonged to the Japanese—China's hated adversaries in the early twentieth century—were not demolished after the 1949 revolution. In fact, the former Japanese legation compound, located just up the street to the left of the bank building, became the Beijing mayor's office. The Grand Hotel des Wagons-Lits, meanwhile, was converted into a government guesthouse in the 1950s. The building was torn down in the early 1980s.

This is a view of the eastern Qianmen train station in the early 1930s. The photograph was taken looking to the southeast from the Qianmen Gate tower. Railroads first appeared in Beijing in the late 1890s as part of the attempt to modernize China's transportation system. The Peking-Mukden Railway, financed and built by the British, entered the city from the east. The Peking-Hankow Railway, financed and built by the French and Belgians, entered the city from the west. These two railways arrived in Beijing along the southern wall of the Inner City, meeting at Qianmen Gate. Separate stations on either side of the gate were built in the early 1900s to accommodate the traffic on these railroads.

This view of the distinctive banded-brick building of the eastern Qianmen train station is taken from the Qianmen Gate tower, the last remaining gate tower in Beijing. Under Japanese occupation (1937–1945), this station was used exclusively for passenger traffic while the station on the west side of the gate was used only for freight traffic. In 1959, a gigantic new train station was built at Chongwenmen, and both of the Qianmen stations ceased operating. The western station was subsequently demolished, while the eastern station pictured here was ultimately converted into a shopping mall. The old train station building was clearly reconfigured at some point after 1945.

Beijing's first McDonald's was located at the northeast corner of Changan and Wangfujing—then and still the most desirable commercial location in the city. This photograph, taken shortly after the restaurant opened in 1992, shows a giant Ronald McDonald figure hovering Buddha-like over the entrance. This was the largest McDonald's in the world, with 700 seats and twenty-nine cash registers. It served 40,000 customers on its first day of business. There are now over a hundred McDonald's in Beijing. In early 2007, the company opened its first drive-through restaurant in the city as part of a joint venture with Sinopec, China's second-largest oil company. These firms plan to build thirty combination drive-through restaurants/gas stations in Beijing by the summer of 2008. Many Chinese are drawn to McDonald's as a symbol of modernization and American culture, but some are concerned that more cars, more emissions, and more fast food are having dire consequences for public health and the environment.

Today, the northeast corner of Wangfujing and Changan is occupied by the 8.6 million-square-foot Oriental Plaza, one of the largest commercial complexes in Asia. This "city-within-a-city" contains eight office buildings, two luxury apartment buildings, a Grand Hyatt hotel, and the Oriental Plaza Mall, Beijing's most posh shopping center. The property was developed by Hong Kong tycoon Li Kai Shing. To make way for the $2 billion project, McDonald's was forced to relocate its flagship restaurant in 1996 despite having a long-term lease on the site. Their new restaurant can be seen just up the street on the right. The Oriental Plaza now dominates the entrance to the pedestrian shopping corridor along Wangfujing Street, the commercial heart of Beijing. The fact that a thriving business was displaced less than five years after opening to make way for a larger venture epitomizes the rapid pace at which global real-estate investment is remaking Beijing's urban landscapes.

Japanese army officers parade down Changan Boulevard in 1937. In the First Sino-Japanese War of 1894–95, China was defeated and was forced to cede Taiwan as well as all claims to Korea. Over the next several decades, Japanese aggression toward China intensified as part of a broader strategy to gain control over mainland Asia. In 1937, Japan invaded China and quickly secured a large section of Chinese territory, including Beijing. Changan is the street that runs east to west through the Inner City, directly in front of Tiananmen Gate. In the background of the photograph is a large pailou, the traditional ceremonial archway placed over important streets. Nearly identical pailou marked the eastern and western entrances to the street.

This view looks eastward along Changan Boulevard at its intersection with Chongwenmenai Boulevard, east of Tiananmen Gate. During the 1950s, when Beijing's road system was rebuilt, Changan was enlarged into a 100-yard-wide thoroughfare with a major streetcar line at its center. The two pailou that stood at either end of the street were removed at that time.

Today, Changan is Beijing's central east–west artery, extending in both directions to the Second and Third Ring roads. The boulevard is now lined with Western-style business towers, government offices, hotels, and shopping centers. This image captures the generally poor air quality that has become all too common in Beijing today.

Also known as the Old Summer Palace, Yuanmingyuan—the Garden of Perfect Purity—was the original summer residence of the Qing emperors. Seen here in the mid-1920s, the Old Summer Palace was a grand landscape of magnificent buildings and beautiful gardens located to the north and west of Beijing. Built over a sixty-year period beginning in 1735, the complex featured both Chinese and European designs. In an unprecedented nod to Western aesthetics, the emperor directed an Italian Jesuit in his court to build a series of Western-style structures, fountains, and gardens in the fashion of Versailles. In the aftermath of the Second Opium War in 1860, British and French forces burned Yuanmingyuan to punish the emperor—but not before plundering the palace and removing nearly everything of value. In the 1920s, the Old Summer Palace remained a ghostly shell of Baroque refinement.

Yuanmingyuan today is a large and very popular public park located in the northwest of Beijing between the Fourth and Fifth Ring roads. The Old Summer Palace complex is full of the ruins of the 1860 burning and looting, just as it was in the 1920s. These ruins have remained in place because they have become important memorials to the indignity of past humiliations perpetrated by foreign invaders. This interpretation of the site is actively promoted by the Chinese government, which is currently debating whether to preserve the ruins or to replace them with a reconstruction of the original Yuanmingyuan palace. In either case, the government will use the site as a symbol of patriotism, intended perhaps in part as a warning about the wave of Western culture currently invading China.

Wanshoushan—Longevity Hill—in 1860. Wanshoushan, which lies just to the west of the Old Summer Palace, had been used as an imperial garden retreat for centuries, but on a much more modest scale than Yuanmingyuan. After the British and French forces burned Yuanmingyuan to the ground during the Second Opium War in 1860, they turned to Wanshoushan and burned it as well. The photograph, by Felice Beato, was taken in the immediate aftermath of the destruction. The view is to the northwest and shows an empty platform and ruins where large temples had previously stood. The building at the top of the hill is the Buddhist Temple of Wisdom, which survived the fire because it was a masonry building. A long marble balustrade and the ruins of a boathouse can be seen along the lakeshore.

The area around Wanshoushan was chosen by Empress Dowager Cixi as the site for a new summer palace in the 1880s. The new palace—named Yiheyuan—centered on Kunming Lake, seen here in the foreground. Yiheyuan covers an area of over 700 acres, three-quarters of which is water. Surrounding the lake, the empress built an extensive and magnificent garden landscape filled with palaces, pavilions, temples, courtyards, and bridges.

The prominent octagonal building on the hill is the Pagoda of Buddhist Virtue, which was rebuilt in 1889. The Temple of Wisdom at the top of the hill features external walls made up of hundreds of colored tiled niches, each filled with a Buddha image. These Buddha figures had their heads removed during the Cultural Revolution.

The New Summer Palace, Yiheyuan, in the mid-1920s. This photograph was taken looking west from the octagonal Pagoda of Buddhist Virtue located on Longevity Hill. On the hill in the distance is the Jade Fountain Pagoda, a hexagonal, seven-story pagoda located in the Imperial Hunting Park. In the foreground on the right is the Pavilion of Precious Clouds, set on a high marble base and framed by walkways and smaller pavilions. This structure is considered to be one of the great achievements of Chinese architecture; though it looks like a wood-and-tile building, the pavilion was made entirely of cast bronze in 1755. The Bronze Pavilion survived the 1860 burning—and the looting that followed the Boxer Rebellion—with minimal damage.

This broad overview has changed little over the last seventy-five years, but the details have changed considerably. The buildings of Yiheyuan have been carefully restored as shown in the flawless tile and meticulous painted woodwork of this group of structures. Yiheyuan, like so many other imperial spaces, was badly neglected during the first half of the twentieth century. Restoration of the complex began soon after the founding of the People's Republic in 1949. The New Summer Palace was designated as a protected cultural site in 1960 and was listed as a UNESCO World Heritage Site in 1998. It is one of Beijing's primary tourist attractions, visited by hundreds of thousands of people each year.

This is the famous Marble Boat at the New Summer Palace, Yiheyuan, in the mid-1920s. The stone boat sits at the north edge of Kunming Lake, a short distance west of the Pagoda of Buddhist Virtue. An original version of the pavilion was built here in 1755 but was destroyed by European troops in 1860. In 1893, Empress Dowager Cixi had the pavilion rebuilt as part of the creation of the New Summer Palace. The pavilion has a marble base on which sits a delicately painted wooden structure. The Marble Boat is often viewed as emblematic of the decay of the Qing Dynasty; the money that built it (and much of the rest of the New Summer Palace) was supposedly taken from funds intended to modernize the imperial navy. China suffered a crushing naval defeat at the hands of the Japanese in 1895.

Today, the Marble Boat—a somewhat incongruous reproduction of a steam paddleboat—appears remarkably out of place amid the composed and harmonious landscape of traditional Chinese garden architecture. The stone boat also seems a bit lonely and neglected; it sits next to Kunming Lake's main boat launch and is overshadowed by the noisy ferries that shuttle tourists on excursions around the lake. Like much of the New Summer Palace, the Marble Boat was damaged by foreign troops in the aftermath of the Boxer Rebellion in 1900. It was promptly repaired by the imperial government in 1902. One can imagine the imperial retinue passing a languid summer afternoon under the painted canopy.

The Jade Belt Bridge at the New Summer Palace, Yiheyuan, in an undated photograph. The Jade Belt Bridge connects two narrow strips of land that run through the western half of Kunming Lake. The bridge is approached from the main Summer Palace complex from the north, on a narrow, willow-lined causeway. It is one of six bridges along this picturesque route. The pedestrian bridge, known widely as the Camel Back Bridge, was built in the eighteenth century. It is made of marble, and its railings are decorated with carved cranes. The graceful arch shape, whose reflection creates a full circle in this photograph, was chosen to allow passage of the emperor's boat.

The western, or "back lake," area of Yiheyuan is one of the most tranquil and elegant parts of the garden complex. This side of the New Summer Palace has considerably fewer structures than the main palace complex on the north side of Kunming Lake. Instead, the focus here is on the narrow paths that wind through dense trees and over delicate bridges. The Jade Belt Bridge is the highlight of the area. It remains one of the most photographed structures in all of Beijing. This photograph was taken from the shore just to the west of the bridge, while the historical photograph on the opposite page was taken from a boat on the water.

This is a view of the Great Wall of China in the 1920s. This defensive fortification along the northern edge of the Chinese Empire was built over a period of two thousand years to protect successive dynasties from northern invaders. The portions of the Great Wall that survive today date mostly from the fifteenth century and reflect the Ming Dynasty's program to extend and reinforce the wall in the face of constant attacks by the Mongols. During the eighteenth century, the wall was neglected and began to decay because the Manchu rulers of the Qing Dynasty were themselves invaders from the north who maintained control over Manchuria. By the early twentieth century, much of the Great Wall had fallen into disrepair. This photograph shows a ruined stretch of wall at Badaling, looking to the east.

The Great Wall is the largest tourist attraction in China and one of the most visited sites in the entire world. An estimated five million people come to the Great Wall each year. Badaling is by far the most popular stretch of the wall; it is located just thirty-five miles north of Beijing and is accessible by an expressway. The Chinese government began to restore sections of the Great Wall in the early 1950s. This section of the wall at Badaling was the first to be restored and was opened to tourists in 1957. The sheer scale and magnitude of the wall is remarkable. One is struck by the massive ongoing investment of resources needed by imperial dynasties, not to mention the current government, to maintain this bulwark. Parts of the wall, even at this heavily visited site, are crumbling. Efforts are ongoing to raise money to maintain this vast and impressive relic.

This is a 1932 photograph of the Great Wall of China at Badaling. The Great Wall of the Ming Dynasty represents the longest man-made structure in the world. It stretches nearly 4,000 miles, from the Pacific Ocean to the deserts of the Tarim Basin in the west. This section of wall near Beijing was the most heavily fortified; the wall was between twenty-five and forty feet high, sixteen feet wide, and marked by guard towers placed regularly along its route. Such an edifice required massive amounts of forced labor over hundreds of years. Ironically, the Ming Dynasty fell when a Ming general opened the gate and allowed the Manchus through. He hoped that they would help quell a peasant rebellion that had emerged in response to harsh treatment by the Ming rulers. Instead, the Manchus invaded Beijing and established their own dynasty. In this photograph, looking east, the Great Wall can be seen snaking along the mountainside into the distance.

Near where this photograph was taken is a tablet inscribed with the words of Mao Zedong. There are many slightly varying translations, but in essence Mao said, "You cannot be a Chinese hero until you've visited the Great Wall." In part because Mao's words have lasting influence in China, and in part because many more Chinese today have the financial means to take vacations, the Great Wall is completely overrun by domestic tourists. First-time Chinese visitors happily purchase their "hero" certificates, attesting that they have made the pilgrimage urged by Mao. A large and growing number of foreign tourists join the Chinese visitors, and the result is a great wall of humanity competing for space atop this historic relic. The motto for the Beijing Olympic Games is prominently displayed on the hillside; given the throngs of tourists at Badaling, it sometimes seems that the world's one dream is to visit the Great Wall all at once.

American President Richard Nixon and Chinese Vice Premier Li Hsiennien smile as they look out over the Great Wall during Nixon's historic visit to China in February of 1972. This was the first time a U.S. president had visited the People's Republic of China. Nixon's meetings with Mao Zedong and Zhou Enlai resulted in the Shanghai Communique, a joint statement on foreign policy that opened the door for economic and cultural contact between the two countries. Given Nixon's fervent anticommunism and Mao's fierce anticapitalist polemics, this first step toward mutual recognition and accommodation shocked the allies and enemies of both nations. The visit eased the hostility between China and the United States and changed the course of twentieth-century geopolitics.

The fact that so many foreign tourists are visible at the Great Wall today is a result of the new direction in the Sino-American relationships initiated by Nixon's historic visit in 1972. It opened doors between China and the West and, perhaps inadvertently, sowed the seeds of China's emergence as a critical player in the global capitalist economy. Neither Nixon nor Mao could have foreseen this dramatic change of course in communist China, nor could they have anticipated that China would be running a $200 billion trade surplus with the United States by the early twenty-first century. China is now flooded with the representatives of U.S. businesses, each seeking to take advantage of economic opportunities that have blossomed in recent years. The Great Wall itself provides ample testament to the Chinese entrepreneurial spirit. One can scarcely walk ten steps without being confronted with yet another opportunity to buy souvenirs.

The entrance to the Ming Tombs in the mid-1920s. The tombs of the Ming emperors are located thirty miles north of Beijing. The site was selected in 1420 according to the traditional principles of feng shui, which dictated that malicious spirits emanating from the north must be deflected. The tombs lie in a quiet valley ringed by mountains that form an arc from the northwest to the northeast, providing the necessary protection from unhealthy influences. Thirteen of the sixteen Ming emperors are buried in this walled complex. The entrance to the tombs is at the southern end of the valley and is marked by a magnificent marble pailou, believed by many to be the most beautiful pailou in all of China. The pailou was erected in 1541.

The area around the entrance to the Ming Tombs has changed dramatically over the past century. Trees have been planted in the valley, and much of the open space surrounding the monuments has been put into agricultural production. Today, the marble pailou no longer functions as the gateway to the tombs; instead, a busy road located just beyond the trees bypasses the archway and carries tourists to the entrance gates of the various tomb sites. In fact, the pailou is unmarked and is barely visible from the road. The structure is also inaccessible; it sits on a dirt side road next to a utility shed, surrounded by a rusted metal fence, neglected and forgotten.

A mile beyond the marble pailou marking the entrance to the Ming Tombs lies the Great Palace Gate, which leads to the Spirit Road, shown here around 1940. This mile-long corridor is lined on both sides with eighteen pairs of stone figures, each one carved out of a single block of limestone. There are lions, camels, elephants, and horses, as well as mythological figures like the xiezhai, a catlike creature with horns. In addition to the animals, there are statues of military and civil dignitaries. It is likely that the animals represented the extent of the empire—camels for the west, elephants for the south, and horses for the north. The human figures represented the imperial court, while the mythological creatures embodied the qualities of peace, justice, and power associated with the emperor. The tombs themselves are located two miles farther north along this path.

The linear path that once led imperial processions along the Spirit Road and through the valley to the tombs has today been completely interrupted. The significant elements of the overall tomb complex are now disconnected and seem to the visitor to be separate sites (with separate entrance fees). The contrast with the landscape of the past is stark. In the 1940s, the valley was barren and austere, lacking any vegetation whatsoever. Now, the panoramic mountain vistas are obscured by a corridor of willow trees that flank the Spirit Road, creating a lush, green environment. The Ming Tombs complex was placed under state protection in 1957. It became a UNESCO World Heritage Site in 2003.

The United States Cavalry, Troop L, on the Spirit Road, around 1900. In the late nineteenth and early twentieth centuries, most foreigners visited the Ming Tombs on their way to or from a tour of the Great Wall of China. Most did not visit the actual tombs but rather focused on the Spirit Road because it was such a unique and dramatic place. The soldiers in the photograph were part of the United States' China Relief Expedition, which stormed the city wall in Beijing, defeated the Boxers, and relieved the foreign population that had been under siege in the Legation Quarter. In addition to their military duties, the soldiers found time for touring. There are also historic photographs of this same group posing in front of the Great Wall.

As in the past, most tourists today visit the Ming Tombs as part of a Great Wall itinerary. They usually arrive at the tombs on a tour bus late in the day, after a strenuous hike along the wall at Badaling. Interestingly, most of the tour buses deposit visitors two miles farther up the valley at the Changling Tomb, burial site of the first Ming emperor to rule from Beijing. Because of the dense vegetation, the imposing statues along the Spirit Road are not visible from the main road. The buses drive right past the Spirit Road, and many visitors end their frenetic day without ever seeing this impressive site.

INDEX